Petty Cash Log

Petty Cash

Time Period: _____   Starting Balance: _____

Date	Disbursed To	Purpose	Approved By	Amount
Total				

Petty Cash

Time Period: _____   Starting Balance: _____

Date	Disbursed To	Purpose	Approved By	Amount
Total				

Petty Cash

Time Period: _____   Starting Balance: _____

Date	Disbursed To	Purpose	Approved By	Amount
Total				

Petty Cash

Time Period: _____   Starting Balance: _____

Date	Disbursed To	Purpose	Approved By	Amount
Total				

Petty Cash

Time Period: _____   Starting Balance: _____

Date	Disbursed To	Purpose	Approved By	Amount
Total				

Petty Cash

Time Period: _____   Starting Balance: _____

Date	Disbursed To	Purpose	Approved By	Amount
Total				

Petty Cash

Time Period: _____   Starting Balance: _____

Date	Disbursed To	Purpose	Approved By	Amount
Total				

Petty Cash

Time Period: _____   Starting Balance: _____

Date	Disbursed To	Purpose	Approved By	Amount
Total				

Petty Cash

Time Period: _____   Starting Balance: _____

Date	Disbursed To	Purpose	Approved By	Amount
Total				

Petty Cash

Time Period: _____   Starting Balance: _____

Date	Disbursed To	Purpose	Approved By	Amount
Total				

Petty Cash

Time Period: _____   Starting Balance: _____

Date	Disbursed To	Purpose	Approved By	Amount
Total				

Petty Cash

Time Period: _____   Starting Balance: _____

Date	Disbursed To	Purpose	Approved By	Amount
Total				

Petty Cash

Time Period: _____   Starting Balance: _____

Date	Disbursed To	Purpose	Approved By	Amount
Total				

Petty Cash

Time Period: _____   Starting Balance: _____

Date	Disbursed To	Purpose	Approved By	Amount
Total				

Petty Cash

Time Period: _____   Starting Balance: _____

Date	Disbursed To	Purpose	Approved By	Amount
Total				

Petty Cash

Time Period: _____   Starting Balance: _____

Date	Disbursed To	Purpose	Approved By	Amount
Total				

Petty Cash

Time Period: _____   Starting Balance: _____

Date	Disbursed To	Purpose	Approved By	Amount
Total				

Petty Cash

Time Period: _____   Starting Balance: _____

Date	Disbursed To	Purpose	Approved By	Amount
Total				

Petty Cash

Time Period: _____   Starting Balance: _____

Date	Disbursed To	Purpose	Approved By	Amount
Total				

Petty Cash

Time Period: _____   Starting Balance: _____

Date	Disbursed To	Purpose	Approved By	Amount
Total				

Petty Cash

Time Period: _____   Starting Balance: _____

Date	Disbursed To	Purpose	Approved By	Amount
Total				

Petty Cash

Time Period: _____   Starting Balance: _____

Date	Disbursed To	Purpose	Approved By	Amount
Total				

Petty Cash

Time Period: _____   Starting Balance: _____

Date	Disbursed To	Purpose	Approved By	Amount
Total				

Petty Cash

Time Period: _____   Starting Balance: _____

Date	Disbursed To	Purpose	Approved By	Amount
Total				

Petty Cash

Time Period: _____   Starting Balance: _____

Date	Disbursed To	Purpose	Approved By	Amount
Total				

Petty Cash

Time Period: _____   Starting Balance: _____

Date	Disbursed To	Purpose	Approved By	Amount
Total				

Petty Cash

Time Period: _____   Starting Balance: _____

Date	Disbursed To	Purpose	Approved By	Amount
Total				

Petty Cash

Time Period: _____   Starting Balance: _____

Date	Disbursed To	Purpose	Approved By	Amount
Total				

Petty Cash

Time Period: _____   Starting Balance: _____

Date	Disbursed To	Purpose	Approved By	Amount
Total				

Petty Cash

Time Period: _____   Starting Balance: _____

Date	Disbursed To	Purpose	Approved By	Amount
Total				

Petty Cash

Time Period: _____   Starting Balance: _____

Date	Disbursed To	Purpose	Approved By	Amount
Total				

Petty Cash

Time Period: _____   Starting Balance: _____

Date	Disbursed To	Purpose	Approved By	Amount
Total				

Petty Cash

Time Period: _____   Starting Balance: _____

Date	Disbursed To	Purpose	Approved By	Amount
Total				

Petty Cash

Time Period: _____   Starting Balance: _____

Date	Disbursed To	Purpose	Approved By	Amount
Total				

Petty Cash

Time Period: _____   Starting Balance: _____

Date	Disbursed To	Purpose	Approved By	Amount
Total				

Petty Cash

Time Period: _____   Starting Balance: _____

Date	Disbursed To	Purpose	Approved By	Amount
Total				

Petty Cash

Time Period: _____   Starting Balance: _____

Date	Disbursed To	Purpose	Approved By	Amount
Total				

Petty Cash

Time Period: _____   Starting Balance: _____

Date	Disbursed To	Purpose	Approved By	Amount
	,			
Total				

Petty Cash

Time Period: _____   Starting Balance: _____

Date	Disbursed To	Purpose	Approved By	Amount
Total				

Petty Cash

Time Period: _____   Starting Balance: _____

Date	Disbursed To	Purpose	Approved By	Amount
Total				

Petty Cash

Time Period: _____   Starting Balance: _____

Date	Disbursed To	Purpose	Approved By	Amount
Total				

Petty Cash

Time Period: _____   Starting Balance: _____

Date	Disbursed To	Purpose	Approved By	Amount
Total				

Petty Cash

Time Period: _____   Starting Balance: _____

Date	Disbursed To	Purpose	Approved By	Amount
Total				

Petty Cash

Time Period: _____   Starting Balance: _____

Date	Disbursed To	Purpose	Approved By	Amount
Total				

Petty Cash

Time Period: _____   Starting Balance: _____

Date	Disbursed To	Purpose	Approved By	Amount
Total				

Petty Cash

Time Period: _____   Starting Balance: _____

Date	Disbursed To	Purpose	Approved By	Amount
Total				

Petty Cash

Time Period: _____   Starting Balance: _____

Date	Disbursed To	Purpose	Approved By	Amount
Total				

Petty Cash

Time Period: _____   Starting Balance: _____

Date	Disbursed To	Purpose	Approved By	Amount
Total				

Petty Cash

Time Period: _____   Starting Balance: _____

Date	Disbursed To	Purpose	Approved By	Amount
Total				

Petty Cash

Time Period: _____   Starting Balance: _____

Date	Disbursed To	Purpose	Approved By	Amount
Total				

Petty Cash

Time Period: _____   Starting Balance: _____

Date	Disbursed To	Purpose	Approved By	Amount
Total				

Petty Cash

Time Period: _____   Starting Balance: _____

Date	Disbursed To	Purpose	Approved By	Amount
Total				

Petty Cash

Time Period: _____   Starting Balance: _____

Date	Disbursed To	Purpose	Approved By	Amount
Total				

Petty Cash

Time Period: _____   Starting Balance: _____

Date	Disbursed To	Purpose	Approved By	Amount
Total				

Petty Cash

Time Period: _____   Starting Balance: _____

Date	Disbursed To	Purpose	Approved By	Amount
Total				

Petty Cash

Time Period: _____   Starting Balance: _____

Date	Disbursed To	Purpose	Approved By	Amount
Total				

Petty Cash

Time Period: _____   Starting Balance: _____

Date	Disbursed To	Purpose	Approved By	Amount
Total				

Petty Cash

Time Period: _____   Starting Balance: _____

Date	Disbursed To	Purpose	Approved By	Amount
Total				

Petty Cash

Time Period: _____   Starting Balance: _____

Date	Disbursed To	Purpose	Approved By	Amount
Total				

Petty Cash

Time Period: _____   Starting Balance: _____

Date	Disbursed To	Purpose	Approved By	Amount
Total				

Petty Cash

Time Period: _____   Starting Balance: _____

Date	Disbursed To	Purpose	Approved By	Amount
Total				

Petty Cash

Time Period: _____   Starting Balance: _____

Date	Disbursed To	Purpose	Approved By	Amount
Total				

Petty Cash

Time Period: _____   Starting Balance: _____

Date	Disbursed To	Purpose	Approved By	Amount
Total				

Petty Cash

Time Period: _____   Starting Balance: _____

Date	Disbursed To	Purpose	Approved By	Amount
Total				

Petty Cash

Time Period: _____   Starting Balance: _____

Date	Disbursed To	Purpose	Approved By	Amount
Total				

Petty Cash

Time Period: _____   Starting Balance: _____

Date	Disbursed To	Purpose	Approved By	Amount
Total				

Petty Cash

Time Period: _____   Starting Balance: _____

Date	Disbursed To	Purpose	Approved By	Amount
Total				

Petty Cash

Time Period: _____   Starting Balance: _____

Date	Disbursed To	Purpose	Approved By	Amount
Total				

Petty Cash

Time Period: _____   Starting Balance: _____

Date	Disbursed To	Purpose	Approved By	Amount
Total				

Petty Cash

Time Period: _____   Starting Balance: _____

Date	Disbursed To	Purpose	Approved By	Amount
Total				

Petty Cash

Time Period: _____   Starting Balance: _____

Date	Disbursed To	Purpose	Approved By	Amount
Total				

Petty Cash

Time Period: _____   Starting Balance: _____

Date	Disbursed To	Purpose	Approved By	Amount
Total				

Petty Cash

Time Period: _____   Starting Balance: _____

Date	Disbursed To	Purpose	Approved By	Amount
Total				

Petty Cash

Time Period: _____   Starting Balance: _____

Date	Disbursed To	Purpose	Approved By	Amount
Total				

Petty Cash

Time Period: _____   Starting Balance: _____

Date	Disbursed To	Purpose	Approved By	Amount
Total				

Petty Cash

Time Period: _____   Starting Balance: _____

Date	Disbursed To	Purpose	Approved By	Amount
Total				

Petty Cash

Time Period: _____   Starting Balance: _____

Date	Disbursed To	Purpose	Approved By	Amount
Total				

Petty Cash

Time Period: _____   Starting Balance: _____

Date	Disbursed To	Purpose	Approved By	Amount
Total				

Petty Cash

Time Period: _____   Starting Balance: _____

Date	Disbursed To	Purpose	Approved By	Amount
Total				

Petty Cash

Time Period: _____   Starting Balance: _____

Date	Disbursed To	Purpose	Approved By	Amount
Total				

Petty Cash

Time Period: _____   Starting Balance: _____

Date	Disbursed To	Purpose	Approved By	Amount
Total				

Petty Cash

Time Period: _____   Starting Balance: _____

Date	Disbursed To	Purpose	Approved By	Amount
Total				

Petty Cash

Time Period: _____   Starting Balance: _____

Date	Disbursed To	Purpose	Approved By	Amount
Total				

Petty Cash

Time Period: _____   Starting Balance: _____

Date	Disbursed To	Purpose	Approved By	Amount
Total				

Petty Cash

Time Period: _____   Starting Balance: _____

Date	Disbursed To	Purpose	Approved By	Amount
Total				

Petty Cash

Time Period: _____   Starting Balance: _____

Date	Disbursed To	Purpose	Approved By	Amount
Total				

Petty Cash

Time Period: _____   Starting Balance: _____

Date	Disbursed To	Purpose	Approved By	Amount
Total				

Petty Cash

Time Period: _____   Starting Balance: _____

Date	Disbursed To	Purpose	Approved By	Amount
Total				

Petty Cash

Time Period: _____   Starting Balance: _____

Date	Disbursed To	Purpose	Approved By	Amount
Total				

Petty Cash

Time Period: _____   Starting Balance: _____

Date	Disbursed To	Purpose	Approved By	Amount
Total				

Petty Cash

Time Period: _____   Starting Balance: _____

Date	Disbursed To	Purpose	Approved By	Amount
Total				

Petty Cash

Time Period: _____   Starting Balance: _____

Date	Disbursed To	Purpose	Approved By	Amount
Total				

Petty Cash

Time Period: _____   Starting Balance: _____

Date	Disbursed To	Purpose	Approved By	Amount
Total				

Petty Cash

Time Period: _____   Starting Balance: _____

Date	Disbursed To	Purpose	Approved By	Amount
Total				

Petty Cash

Time Period: _____   Starting Balance: _____

Date	Disbursed To	Purpose	Approved By	Amount
Total				

Petty Cash

Time Period: _____   Starting Balance: _____

Date	Disbursed To	Purpose	Approved By	Amount
Total				

Petty Cash

Time Period: _____   Starting Balance: _____

Date	Disbursed To	Purpose	Approved By	Amount
Total				

Petty Cash

Time Period: _____   Starting Balance: _____

Date	Disbursed To	Purpose	Approved By	Amount
Total				

Petty Cash

Time Period: _____   Starting Balance: _____

Date	Disbursed To	Purpose	Approved By	Amount
Total				

Petty Cash

Time Period: _____   Starting Balance: _____

Date	Disbursed To	Purpose	Approved By	Amount
Total				

Petty Cash

Time Period: _____   Starting Balance: _____

Date	Disbursed To	Purpose	Approved By	Amount
Total				

Petty Cash

Time Period: _____   Starting Balance: _____

Date	Disbursed To	Purpose	Approved By	Amount
Total				

Petty Cash

Time Period: _____   Starting Balance: _____

Date	Disbursed To	Purpose	Approved By	Amount
Total				

Petty Cash

Time Period: _____   Starting Balance: _____

Date	Disbursed To	Purpose	Approved By	Amount
Total				

Petty Cash

Time Period: _____   Starting Balance: _____

Date	Disbursed To	Purpose	Approved By	Amount
Total				

Petty Cash

Time Period: _____   Starting Balance: _____

Date	Disbursed To	Purpose	Approved By	Amount
Total				

Petty Cash

Time Period: _____   Starting Balance: _____

Date	Disbursed To	Purpose	Approved By	Amount
Total				

Petty Cash

Time Period: _____   Starting Balance: _____

Date	Disbursed To	Purpose	Approved By	Amount
Total				

Petty Cash

Time Period: _____   Starting Balance: _____

Date	Disbursed To	Purpose	Approved By	Amount
Total				

Petty Cash

Time Period: _____   Starting Balance: _____

Date	Disbursed To	Purpose	Approved By	Amount
Total				

Petty Cash

Time Period: _____   Starting Balance: _____

Date	Disbursed To	Purpose	Approved By	Amount
Total				

Petty Cash

Time Period: _____   Starting Balance: _____

Date	Disbursed To	Purpose	Approved By	Amount
Total				

Petty Cash

Time Period: _____   Starting Balance: _____

Date	Disbursed To	Purpose	Approved By	Amount
Total				

Petty Cash

Time Period: _____   Starting Balance: _____

Date	Disbursed To	Purpose	Approved By	Amount
Total				

Petty Cash

Time Period: _____   Starting Balance: _____

Date	Disbursed To	Purpose	Approved By	Amount
Total				

Petty Cash

Time Period: _____   Starting Balance: _____

Date	Disbursed To	Purpose	Approved By	Amount
Total				

Petty Cash

Time Period: _____   Starting Balance: _____

Date	Disbursed To	Purpose	Approved By	Amount
Total				

Petty Cash

Time Period: _____   Starting Balance: _____

Date	Disbursed To	Purpose	Approved By	Amount
Total				

Petty Cash

Time Period: _____   Starting Balance: _____

Date	Disbursed To	Purpose	Approved By	Amount
Total				

Petty Cash

Time Period: _____   Starting Balance: _____

Date	Disbursed To	Purpose	Approved By	Amount
Total				

Petty Cash

Time Period: _____   Starting Balance: _____

Date	Disbursed To	Purpose	Approved By	Amount
Total				

Petty Cash

Time Period: _____   Starting Balance: _____

Date	Disbursed To	Purpose	Approved By	Amount
Total				

Petty Cash

Time Period: _____   Starting Balance: _____

Date	Disbursed To	Purpose	Approved By	Amount
Total				

Petty Cash

Time Period: _____   Starting Balance: _____

Date	Disbursed To	Purpose	Approved By	Amount
Total				

Petty Cash

Time Period: _____   Starting Balance: _____

Date	Disbursed To	Purpose	Approved By	Amount
Total				

Petty Cash

Time Period: _____   Starting Balance: _____

Date	Disbursed To	Purpose	Approved By	Amount
Total				

Petty Cash

Time Period: _____   Starting Balance: _____

Date	Disbursed To	Purpose	Approved By	Amount
Total				

Petty Cash

Time Period: _____   Starting Balance: _____

Date	Disbursed To	Purpose	Approved By	Amount
Total				

Petty Cash

Time Period: _____   Starting Balance: _____

Date	Disbursed To	Purpose	Approved By	Amount
Total				

Petty Cash

Time Period: _____   Starting Balance: _____

Date	Disbursed To	Purpose	Approved By	Amount
Total				

Petty Cash

Time Period: _____   Starting Balance: _____

Date	Disbursed To	Purpose	Approved By	Amount
Total				

Petty Cash

Time Period: _____   Starting Balance: _____

Date	Disbursed To	Purpose	Approved By	Amount
Total				

Petty Cash

Time Period: _____   Starting Balance: _____

Date	Disbursed To	Purpose	Approved By	Amount
Total				

Petty Cash

Time Period: _____   Starting Balance: _____

Date	Disbursed To	Purpose	Approved By	Amount
Total				

Petty Cash

Time Period: _____   Starting Balance: _____

Date	Disbursed To	Purpose	Approved By	Amount
Total				

Petty Cash

Time Period: _____   Starting Balance: _____

Date	Disbursed To	Purpose	Approved By	Amount
Total				

Petty Cash

Time Period: _____   Starting Balance: _____

Date	Disbursed To	Purpose	Approved By	Amount
Total				

Petty Cash

Time Period: _____   Starting Balance: _____

Date	Disbursed To	Purpose	Approved By	Amount
Total				

Petty Cash

Time Period: _____   Starting Balance: _____

Date	Disbursed To	Purpose	Approved By	Amount
Total				

Petty Cash

Time Period: _____   Starting Balance: _____

Date	Disbursed To	Purpose	Approved By	Amount
Total				

Petty Cash

Time Period: _____   Starting Balance: _____

Date	Disbursed To	Purpose	Approved By	Amount
Total				

Petty Cash

Time Period: _____   Starting Balance: _____

Date	Disbursed To	Purpose	Approved By	Amount
Total				

Petty Cash

Time Period: _____   Starting Balance: _____

Date	Disbursed To	Purpose	Approved By	Amount
Total				

Petty Cash

Time Period: _____   Starting Balance: _____

Date	Disbursed To	Purpose	Approved By	Amount
Total				

Petty Cash

Time Period: _____   Starting Balance: _____

Date	Disbursed To	Purpose	Approved By	Amount
Total				

Petty Cash

Time Period: _____   Starting Balance: _____

Date	Disbursed To	Purpose	Approved By	Amount
Total				

Petty Cash

Time Period: _____   Starting Balance: _____

Date	Disbursed To	Purpose	Approved By	Amount
Total				

Petty Cash

Time Period: _____   Starting Balance: _____

Date	Disbursed To	Purpose	Approved By	Amount
Total				

Petty Cash

Time Period: _____   Starting Balance: _____

Date	Disbursed To	Purpose	Approved By	Amount
Total				

Petty Cash

Time Period: _____   Starting Balance: _____

Date	Disbursed To	Purpose	Approved By	Amount
Total				

Petty Cash

Time Period: _____   Starting Balance: _____

Date	Disbursed To	Purpose	Approved By	Amount
Total				